Doing nice things for other people for no reason at all is called Philanthropy.

Dedicated to JWH - the biggest-hearted person we know. We love you!

Lots of love to Tim, Jackson, Barbara, Debbie, Justin & Anne. Thanks, guys!

Printed in Canada.
Manufactured by Friesens Corporation.
Manufactured in Altona, MB, Canada in July, 2010.
Job # 126173
ISBN 978-1-935497-20-2

Published by:
Butler Books
P.O. Box 7311
Louisville, KY 40207
(502) 897-9393
Fax (502) 897-9797
www.butlerbooks.com

Butler Books

The initial publication of this book was made possible by a generous grant from The Community Foundation of Louisville, Louisville, Kentucky.

PHILANTHROPY...

a big word for big-hearted people

Written by Jan Helson and Rachel Annette Helson
Illustrated by Rachel Annette Helson

BHP™ ♥ ♥ ♥ A Big-Hearted People™ Publication

PEOPLE

PHILANTHROPY

BIG PEOPLE...AND

LITTLE PEOPLE...

ALL PEOPLE CAN MAKE A DIFFERENCE.

There was a boy, thirteen years old,
Who reviewed the books that authors sold.

Seth Cassel was his name
And helping kids brought him his fame.

Flamingnet, his cool website,
Sold books online both day and night.

With money from his online store,
He bought new books to give libraries more.

So Seth gave stories of animals and toys
To different towns, so girls and boys

Could have some fun and learn new things,
And feel the joy that knowledge brings.

P **H**ELP
I
L
A
N
T
H
R
O
P
Y

THERE ARE A LOT OF WAYS TO **HELP PEOPLE**.

Music and art can be a cure
To some people who think they cannot endure.

It brings joy and laughter, a smile or tear,
But can it help kids be good people all year?

Believe it or not, a young artist and dancer,
Thought he could use peace and love as an answer.

Blake Stuerman helped with workshops to show every kid,
Instead of doing something their parents forbid,

They could dance, sing and paint or even act funny
To help them feel better and make their days sunny.

P
H **I**MPORTANT
I
L
A
N
T
H
R
O
P
Y

IT IS **IMPORTANT** TO REACH OUT
AND **HELP PEOPLE.**

On Thanksgiving, most people eat turkeys and pies,
And think about Pilgrims and Indian guys.

But Hannah Turner helped her family to feed
Those who didn't have food and were in great need.

Hannah noticed a man who sat down to eat,
But he didn't have any socks on his feet.

Even though Hannah was just four years old,
She gave him her socks so his feet wouldn't be cold.

Now "Hannah's Socks" is a big organization,
That gives socks to cold feet throughout the nation.

PHILANTHROPY

LOVE

LOVE IS ONE OF THE MOST IMPORTANT WAYS THAT YOU CAN HELP PEOPLE. LOVE IS

There are kids in the world who do not have houses,
Not much to eat, warm water or blouses.

And then there are some who are given much,
Who share their food and coats and such.

A boy, four years old, named Xavier May,
Proved very young people can help save the day.

With "Meals on Wheels" he delivers food to the old,
In the rain and the sun and the heat and the cold.

PHILANTHROPY

ACT

DO SOMETHING IMPORTANT.
ACT NOW AND HELP PEOPLE
KNOW THAT YOU LOVE THEM.

Talia Leman, a girl of ten,
Gave New Orleans a big ol' grin,

When she started "Random Kid,"
A group to help the ones who did

Say goodbye to their fair city
When Hurricane Katrina wasn't pretty.

At Halloween, she gathered friends
And said, "What if tradition ends?

Instead of asking for treats and candy
Wouldn't dollar bills be dandy?

To share with every New Orleans pal
To rebuild their homes and boost their morale?"

TRICK
or
TREAT!

PHILANTHROPY

NEED

IT IS **IMPORTANT** TO **LOVE** **PEOPLE.**
THEY **NEED** TO KNOW THAT YOU WILL
HELP THEM WITH **ACT**S OF KINDNESS.

Tourette's is a sickness that makes girls and boys
Move in weird ways and make funny noise.

These boys and girls can't help that they're sick,
But often are people the bullies will pick.

Jaylen Arnold, age eight, was one of those boys,
That move in weird ways and make funny noise.

When bullies in school made fun of him badly,
It made him feel hurt and walk around sadly.

Except that, one day, he stood up and said,
"I won't let bullies get into my head!

I'll start a group that will let people know
How bullies can make kids like me feel so low."

And with "Jaylen's Challenge," awareness was raised,
Leaving all who made fun of him changed and amazed.

PHILANTHROPY

TALENT

USE YOUR SPECIAL **TALENT** TO SHOW YOUR **LOVE** TOWARD **PEOPLE** IN **NEED**. **ACT** TO **HELP** THEM KNOW THAT THEY ARE **IMPORTANT**.

Michala Riggle, a girl ten years old,
Helped kids with the beautiful bracelets she sold.

She beaded these bracelets so she could help pay
For a medical treatment that wise doctors say

Helps autistic kids like Evan, her brother,
Who want to get better, one way or another.

PHILANTHROPY

Heart

IT IS **IMPORTANT** TO **ACT** TO **HELP** MANY **PEOPLE**. IF YOU ARE KIND TO OTHERS IN **NEED** AND SHARE YOUR **TALENTS**, IT WILL FILL YOUR **HEART** WITH **LOVE**.

Some children have long hair, curly and thick,
And then some have short hair, glossy and slick,

But when children have cancer they lose all their hair,
And their girl and boy heads are all shiny and bare.

Yet there are good people in this big old world
Who give up their hair to be cut, washed and curled

And made into wigs for the sick kids to wear
To remind the kids to never ever despair.

Lots of cool people want them to get better,
Like Franzi Economy, a first-class go getter!

She was just eight when she cut her blonde locks
For kids in need, because she really rocks!

Ten inches she cut, an amount rather long,
To help a sick child feel happy and strong.

PHILANTHROPY

YOUR ACTIONS CAN MAKE PEOPLE FEEL IMPORTANT. WE ALL HAVE A RESPONSIBILITY TO USE OUR TALENTS TO HELP IMPROVE THE WORLD. WE ALL NEED TO KNOW IN OUR HEART THAT SOMEBODY LOVES US.

RESPONSIBILITY

Frances Cohen, age four, a girl from Kentucky,
Made a cute golden dog extremely lucky.

This dog was a stray who needed an owner
So Frances and family adopted this loner.

She named the dog Davis and gave him a home,
Cleaned him and brushed him with soap and a comb.

Because he had put her under his spell,
She took him to the doctor to make him all well.

So, this little girl, loving and sweet,
Cared for her friend and took him off of the street.

FIRST AID

CLEAN
BILL OF
HEALTH

PHILANTHROPY

OPEN

OPEN YOUR HEART AND SHARE YOUR TALENTS TO HELP PEOPLE IN NEED TO KNOW THEY ARE IMPORTANT. WE ALL HAVE A RESPONSIBILITY TO ACT NOW TO SPREAD LOVE.

When soldiers go fight for the U-S of A,
It is often too hard to find money to pay

For phone calls to family at home overseas.
Not even if soldiers politely ask please!

When Robbie and Brittany Bergquist heard this,
"How awful!," they thought. "How soldiers must miss

Their families at home. But what can we do?
To help them from feeling so lonely and blue?

We'll ask for old cell phones from neighbors and mentors
And sell them to all the recycling centers!

And with all that money from selling each phone,
We'll buy calling cards for each soldier to own."

Did they buy the cards? Oh yes! Yes they did!
So soldiers could call wives, parents and kids!

P H I L A N T H R O P Y

Possible

IF YOU HAVE LOVE IN YOUR HEART FOR **PEOPLE** IN **NEED**, IT IS POSSIBLE THAT YOUR KINDESS CAN MAKE A DIFFERENCE. IT IS IMPORTANT TO ACT NOW AND USE YOUR **TALENT**S TO GET INVOLVED. WE ALL HAVE A **RESPONSIBILITY** TO HELP MAKE THE WORLD A BETTER PLACE.

Presents on birthdays are very exciting,
As well as the people you plan on inviting.

On the day Camille Thoms turned eight years old,
She did not want dolls with hair shiny and gold.

Rather than asking for gifts for her room,
Make-up, nail polish or a fancy costume,

She asked her friends to donate her toys
To an after-school program that helps girls and boys.

These children have things called "behavioral issues,"
That make them run wild and rip up their tissues.

But just because children sometimes act bad,
They still need to play so they don't get too sad.

Now all the kids there - each and every one,
Can play with cool stuff and have lots of fun.

PHILANTHROPY You

YOU ARE A SPECIAL PERSON...

YOU CAN MAKE A DIFFERENCE...

What have you done that is **philanthropy**?
Write it down here, for all to see.

PEOPLE
HELP
IMPORTANT
LOVE
ACT
NEED
TALENT
HEART
RESPONSIBILITY
OPEN
POSSIBLE
YOU

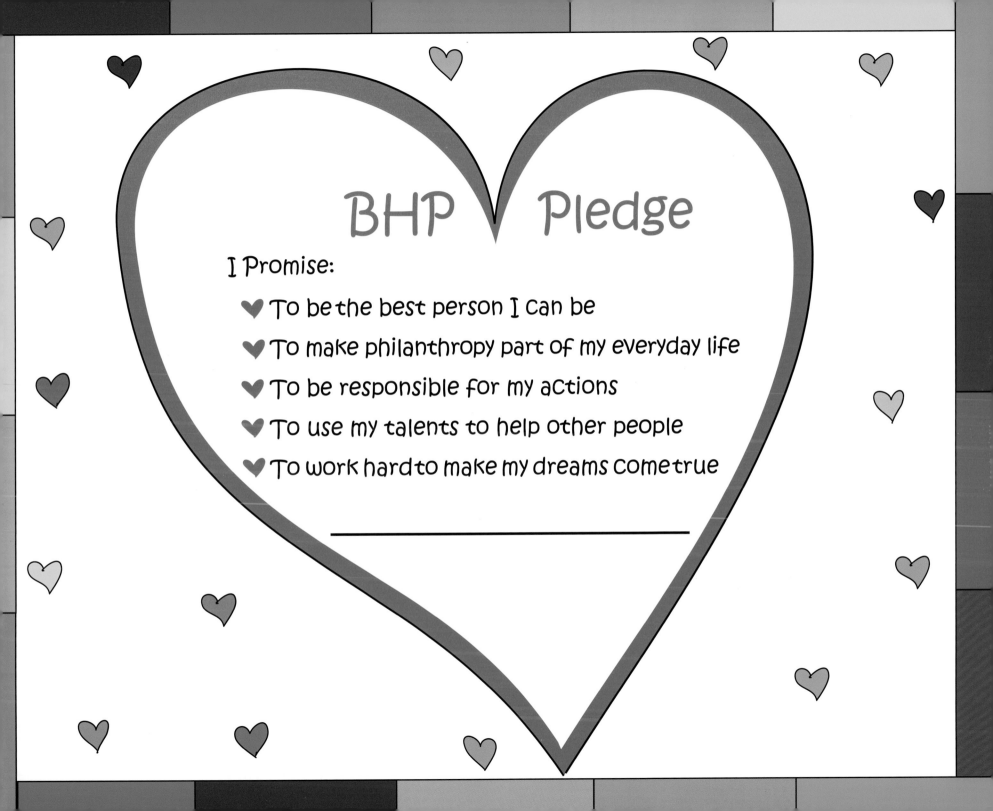

BHP ♥ Pledge

I Promise:

- ♥ To be the best person I can be
- ♥ To make philanthropy part of my everyday life
- ♥ To be responsible for my actions
- ♥ To use my talents to help other people
- ♥ To work hard to make my dreams come true

_____

Mother and daughter, Jan and Rachel Helson, know that kids with **BIG HEARTS** can make a **BIG DIFFERENCE**!

In their book, *PHILANTHROPY...a big word for big-hearted people*, they share inspiring real-life stories of young, Big-Hearted People (BHP), who have done amazing philanthropic work. In this fun-filled and emotional exploration of the word **"PHILANTHROPY"** and the trail-blazing kids who bring the word to life, young readers are encouraged to make philanthropy a part of their lives at an early age. The message: It is never too soon to combine your talents and your compassion to become a philanthropist – and a BHP forever!

A portion of the proceeds from each book purchase will go to support **Blessings in a Backpack**, an organization fighting child hunger and improving educational success. **Blessings in a Backpack** is a unique program designed for children of families that qualify for the federal free and reduced meal program. Blessings provides those children with food for the weekends, at home, transported in a reusable backpack. Jan and Rachel are committed to supporting this organization and, by buying this book, you have joined other **BHP** in doing so as well.

About the authors:

Jan Helson is a successful and innovative entrepreneur and a dedicated philanthropist who with her husband, Tim, has proudly raised two wonderful Big-Hearted kids, Rachel and Jackson, to be the best they can be. Jan lives in Louisville, Kentucky with her family.

Rachel Annette Helson is an actor, writer, producer and philanthropist. She is a recent graduate of NYU's Tisch School of the Arts. Rachel has worked both on and off Broadway as an actress and producer. In 2009, she became the youngest Broadway producer in history to be nominated for a TONY Award. She has raised over $100,000 for her philanthropic causes. Rachel recently moved to Los Angeles, California. Visit www.rachelannettehelson.com for more information about Rachel.

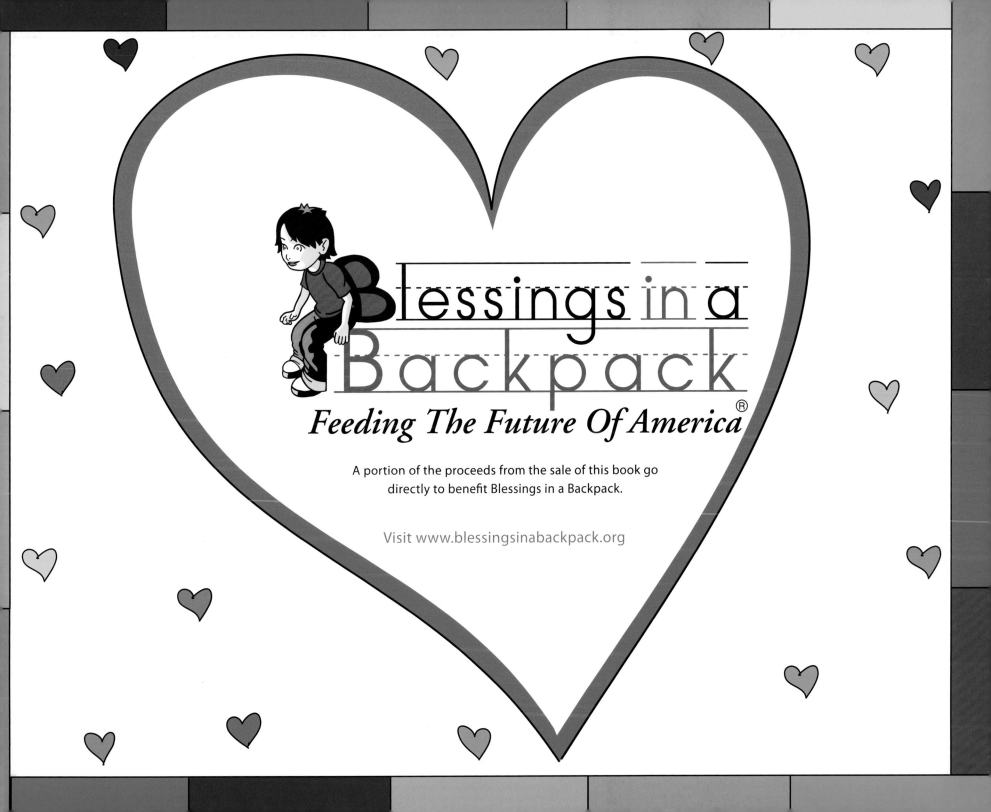

Blessings in a Backpack

Feeding The Future Of America®

A portion of the proceeds from the sale of this book go directly to benefit Blessings in a Backpack.

Visit www.blessingsinabackpack.org

Doing nice things for other people for no reason at all is called Philanthropy.